D1297298

THE UP-COUNTRY LINE

The graceful "Franconia," shown here at Plymouth, N. H., was one of the few engines built by the famous clipper ship builders, McKay & Aldus.
Railway & Locomotive Historical Society

EDGAR T. MEAD

THE UP-COUNTRY LINE

Boston, Concord & Montreal RR
to the New Hampshire Lakes
and White Mountains

SHORTLINE
RR
SERIES

THE
STEPHEN
GREENE
PRESS

Brattleboro   Vermont

This book is dedicated to Malcolm

SPECIAL NOTE TO MODELERS: Several commercial kits are available in HO gauge resembling Boston, Concord & Montreal RR pre-Civil War engines and cars. The popular Virginia & Truckee RR *Genoa,* for example, is not unlike BC&M's *Chocorua,* even to bearing the same number 12. Since almost no two BC&M engines were alike, considerable variety is possible. A model layout might envisage the BC&M mainline from Concord to Woodsville, with a return loop via the Connecticut & Passumpsic and Northern RRs. Scenic possibilities of the mountains are infinite, and advanced modelers will want to add narrow-gauge, logging and cog railroad branches.

Copyright © 1975 by Edgar T. Mead

This book has been produced in the United States of America: designed by R. Dike Hamilton, composed, printed and bound by Halliday Lithograph Corporation. It is published by The Stephen Greene Press, Brattleboro, Vermont 05301.

Library of Congress Cataloging in Publication Data

Mead, Edgar Thorn
    The up-country line.

(Shortline railroad series)
1. Boston, Concord, and Montreal Railroad Company—History
2. Railroads—New Hampshire—History. I. Title.
HE2791.C8722 1975   385'.09742   74-27457
ISBN 0-8289-0248-8

75 76 77 78 79 80 81 9 8 7 6 5 4 3 2 1

FOREWORD

THIS IS A STORY about a tough old New Hampshire railroad, the Boston, Concord & Montreal. During its long life, it was wheeled and dealt, merged and leased, fought over, competed with, bailed out and dismembered. Despite the extinction of its corporate name, it limped along so that physical parts continue to this very moment. If you know where to look, giant GP-6 diesels haul time freights up 2% grades. A former affiliate, the Mt. Washington Railroad, still operates regularly scheduled passenger trains with coal-burning steam locomotives. It controlled or operated trains with five different track gauges, an interurban electric railway, a local streetcar line, steamboats, three unusual hotels, a water aqueduct, logging railroads, a horse-drawn stagecoach line, and a mountain cogwheel railroad. For plausible reasons, it remained a wood-burning railroad long after others had converted to coal. Its steeply graded track became both its charm and its downfall.

Our story chiefly concerns the Boston, Concord & Montreal RR (1842–1895). In so doing it has been the devil's own job not to ramble too far afield on fascinating nearby subjects such as the Concord RR, the Boston & Lowell, and other elements of the once-prosperous Boston & Maine. Credit must be given to the "Rosetta Stone" of the BC&M, a series of newspaper columns by the late Mr. C. E. Caswell of Warren, N.H., who in 1919 had the wit to interview BC&M men then in their 80's and 90's. I have been assisted by the libraries at Concord, N.H., Laconia, N.H., University of New Hampshire and Dartmouth College, also by Walter Wright, Doran Jones, John R. Brennen and Sherman Adams.

There is a fine dry wit in New Hampshire, the humor of the small town farmer who always gets the best of the city slicker. About the time our story begins, an old New Hampshire man stopped in the ticket office at Sanbornton Bridge (now Tilton). How much to Littleton? he asked. That'd be two dollars. Well, now, he went on, how much for a cow or a pig? The cow would be three dollars and the pig one dollar. All right enough, said the farmer, book me as a pig.

Edgar T. Mead

One of two identified railroads on this fragment of an 1862 atlas map is BC&M.
Our story starts at Woodsville, opposite Wells River on the Connecticut River.
R. Dike Hamilton

THE UP-COUNTRY LINE

I

WOODSVILLE. FEBRUARY 5, 1857. It's 6:30 A.M., 15 degrees below zero, heaps of snow on the ground just as in any cold New Hampshire winter. Today there is a BC&M stockholders' meeting in Concord, and we're going to go. Let's find the "Stockholder Special."

North and just across the tracks are a wooden, roofed-over engine house, a long woodshed, and further to the east a car house where passenger cars are stored for the night. Two round-roof coaches and a baggage car all painted yellow have been backed up to the station platform by a high wheel engine, and just now we can see the name on the cab side. It is the *James N. Elkins,* a pet passenger engine on the Boston, Concord & Montreal RR. On another track we can see *Chocorua,* engine-man Henry Little's high-wheel favorite being polished, oiled and "wooded up" for the regular "down" morning passenger train. Every engine has a name up here, sometimes unprintable. For formal purposes anyway, they are named after railroad officials, mountains and towns.

Elkins was built as a passenger engine by Hinkley and Drury's Boston Locomotive Company. Weighing less than freight engines *Pehaungun* or *Winnipiseogee,* its drive wheels are all of six inches larger in diameter. Completed September 12, 1853, the *Elkins'* cylinders and mainrods are *inside* the frames. From a graceful smokestack, gray-white wood smoke pours forth in enormous volume. An arched wire screen covers the funnel as a precaution against sparks setting fire to buildings, bridges and the surrounding forests. However, with the steam blower turned on, small sparks do escape, and ladies and gentlemen with their best winter hats and coats tend to stand well away. The name of Mr. Elkins, first superintendent of the company, is painted in gold with red relief on a letterboard just beneath the cab windows. The initials "B C & M R R" are large on the tender side. Polished brass bands surround the boiler, and brasswork of the running gear gleams even in the cloudy morning light. Atop the boiler is a silver-toned bell.

The wood fire pops and sizzles inside the firebox. A leak of steam from the safety valve sputters and rises aloft in a high white plume. Hiram Judkins, our engineer, walks around the engine carefully inspecting; the severe cold has a way of causing cracks in vital areas. Constant vigilance is necessary. Fireman Albert Keniston, born on a farm and now finishing his apprenticeship as "tallowpot," fills a canister on each of the two cylinders with a pint of tallow, which will drip slowly into the valves and pistons for lubrication.

Mr. Asa Sinclair, our conductor, bids a jovial good morning to the handful of persons boarding for the long trip to the special meeting at Concord. John Cleveland, a youth from one of the extensive farms around Haverhill, N.H., is brakeman, and before the day is over he will have fully earned his dollar and a quarter. He came on duty at five this morning, lit the big wood stoves in the middle of the coaches and two of the smelly spermacetti oil lamps at the ends of the cars. No employee of the BC&M wears a uniform of any kind; only hat badges distinguish the conductors.

At 6:45 Mr. Sinclair shuts his turnip watch with an audible click and waves a go-ahead signal to our engineer. Keniston is still on the ground, ready to shut off the cylinder drain cocks after a few turns of the drive wheels have cleared the cylinders. He will hop back "on the fly." Courtesy of Superintendent Whiton, who will join us at the road's headquarters in Plymouth, we are going to ride the cab part way. Like all wood burners the *Elkins'* exhaust makes a "whoosh-whoosh" sound. Some BC&M engines even tend to make giant smoke rings. *Elkins* starts easily with only three cars to pull. Atop the boiler is a large round brass steam gauge which shows 125 pounds, the working pressure. The engine has been simmering overnight, and the try cocks show that boiler water is low, so Mr. Judkins turns a bypass valve to allow the plunger pumps to fill the boiler. He has the valve marked with file cuts to show full open, half open, and quarter open, and he also has a "pet" position which he has found through experience will allow the pumps to inject as much water as the engine consumes, and no more. He grips the throttle arm tightly; it is not "balanced" and has a tendency to close itself if unattended. Attached to the throttle arm is a threaded wheel which can be tightened to hold the arm at any desired position.

The wood burner chuffs along slowly through the packed snow. Our engineer watches carefully to make sure the stub switch is turned for the BC&M line. The little White Mountains RR branches off here to follow the Ammonoosuc River to Littleton. This line once had a tiny engine, the *Rein Deer*, but now rents the BC&M *Peter Clark* and BC&M cars.

We safely negotiate the switch and begin to pick up speed along a short incline. To the right the Connecticut River meanders through wide, fertile

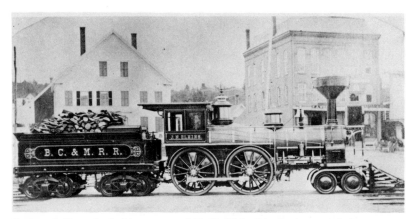

Sleek and shiny, the inside-connected "J. N. Elkins" looks the model of a pre-Civil War passenger engine, shown here at Littleton. *Walker Collection*

pastures that helped Haverhill become the "cow town" of New Hampshire. On this northern end of the BC&M, the track is of better quality than down below, but the rail lengths are only 17 feet. Even at low speed the loud and frequent clicking and clattering make us think we are moving at great speed. Rail joints consist of a 30-inch oak piece outside, bolted through the rail to an iron fishplate inside.

Benefitting from a few hundred rods of level track here, our fireman opens the door and bails in wood as fast as he can. The trick is to select a few chunks of good, dry wood along with the soft "punk" that forms part of every woodpile. In addition to clean-burning hardwoods, there is pine, which burns hot but fast, and cut-off sleepers, or crossties, which are often wet and partly decomposed. You can always tell a new fireman by his bruised and swollen fingers, victims of misaim when throwing a heavy chunk of wood through the firedoor. Sleeper replacement is becoming a serious expense. Local wood tends to rot within a few years so that old sleepers, cut in two, are an undependable source of engine fuel. (It is always an "engine," never a "locomotive," here on the BC&M.)

The exhaust becomes more distinct as we climb upgrade to North Haverhill, now reaching a level high enough to look across the Connecticut River Ox-bow and the Horse Meadows to the west. Looking back along the right side of the train, we see that Mr. Sinclair has "set his target," a BC&M innovation to inform an engineer about the next station stop. The targets are simply wood boards hinged to the coach sides and which can be extended or withdrawn from within the car. At Haverhill Station, located on a curve, brakeman Cleveland can be seen on the front platform of the first coach, watching for signs from the engine that steam has been shut off. The engine and cars come to a stop right at the station. A delegation of 15 people, all stockholders, get on at Haverhill, led by Zanes Clement, one of the original directors. BC&M was conceived in Haverhill; its largest stockholders are here. The 25 original incorporators envisioned a railroad between Boston and Montreal *via* Concord. Connecticut and Passumpsic RR, however, built sooner and quicker up the valley to St. Johnsbury and Lyndonville. Concern is written on Haverhill faces. A business depression has settled on the country. The money market grows tighter by the moment. Creditors are increasingly restless. The Concord RR, the Boston and Lowell RR and the lines over east through the well-established and popular coastal towns seem profitable enough, but the marginal inland roads are in trouble. The financial crisis to be discussed at Concord is only heightened by news that BC&M's Lake Village shops and engine house have burned. Under stovepipe hats and fur collars lurks deep apprehension.

Our train picks up speed again and glides downgrade toward Pike, where we begin the ascent up Oliverian Brook bounding through a narrowing of the valley. Hewn sleepers along the right of way remind us of the many farmer stockholders who have paid for their securities in the currency of crossties, fence posts and fuel wood. We rumble through a wooden covered bridge, then through a rock cut, puffing rapidly to surmount a slight rise. Ahead and to the left we see Black Mountain and just beyond, Moose Hillock, or Moosilauke, standing 4810 feet above sea level and majestically dominating the topography of this region. Its summit and

Flanked by towering Mt. Moosilauke, "Plymouth" tarries awhile with her train bound for Concord and down country. *Railway & Locomotive Historical Soc.*

sides are deep in snow. A carriage road has been widened so that, in summertime, stages can take visitors to the top from Warren Station.

Elkins settles into a slow but steady pace on this slight upgrade. The fireman throws another wet sawed-off sleeper into the firebox, picks up a pot of tallow, and climbs through the cab front door to refill the cylinder cups. To check the boiler water level, the engineer opens try cocks on the boiler and sees that the plunger pumps are keeping water at a desired level. That the *Elkins* runs so evenly and smoothly is a tribute to the inside connection of rods and cylinders, difficult to lubricate and maintain, but causing less oscillation than outside-connected engines. Past East Haverhill, the grade becomes steeper. We approach Warren Summit, which at 1063 feet is the divide between Oliverian Brook and Baker River. Here the roadbed cuts across a root of Moosilauke between Owl's Head and Webster Mountain. Our brakeman has by now taken up his post at the forward brakewheel. The fireman returns from his cylinder oiling and takes up the slack on the tender brake. Our engine has no power brakes and, except for slow leisurely switching in the yard, a stop by reversing risks blowing out a cylinder head. Steam is shut off, and the engine drifts gently over the summit and down through a ¾-mile-long deep cut. This, the major engineering feature of the BC&M, cost $150,000 to build and the life of a workman who died when a black-powder charge exploded prematurely. The sounds of rod motion and wheel clicks echo back and forth down the cut, 60 feet deep in places. There is a clear spring emanating from one side through the ice and snow, a welcome stop for summertime track workers ever since the early days of construction. Our brakeman sets the brake on the rear car, tightening and loosening according to the steepness. Minutes later we arrive at Warren, terminus of the BC&M from 1850 to 1852 when money ran short before the great cut was finally pierced.

All around are stumps of great hemlock and spruce trees. The loggers have cut further and further up the high mountains until there is only a monk's tonsure left. Steam sawmills in Warren cut boards, staves, shingles, and heavy beams for customers such as the shipyards. The largest woodsheds, 95 feet long, are at Warren. We stop to "wood up," and hope to find a few free-riding pass holders who are obliged to help load wood. We take on five cords, each cord a pile eight feet high by eight feet long cut into two-foot lengths.

At Warren we are down on the "third Division" of the BC&M, laid with 50 lb. per yard rail made in England and brought over by clipper ship—all except for 350 tons which sank in a storm off Minot's Ledge, resulting in a $3000 insurance profit. Because of alternate hard and soft spots in the rail, the company has hired a gang of blacksmiths to hammer the rails back to the desired contour. Sidetracks full of platform cars are piled high with lumber bound for outside markets. Several stockholders clamber on board for the free trip to Concord.

South of Warren are more frequent road crossings. The standard signal is a long blast, although at times the engineer adds a toot or two as his personal signature. Up here, the engineer is king. He is assigned an engine and even works on it at the repair shop.

Below Wentworth and Rumney are seven miles of absolutely dead straight track, said to be the longest tangent on any New Hampshire railroad. John McDuffie of Concord surveyed the BC&M, and his experience in canal building shows in the levelness of the BC&M line along Baker River. In tribute to him, there is a freight engine named *McDuffie*.

Toward the end of this long tangent we approach the home, "Quincy House," of Josiah Quincy, BC&M president. At the road crossing is a flag station named "Quincy," and there is Mr. Quincy himself, waiting for the train, nervously discussing prospects with a handful of worried stockholders. To judge from the frown on his face, we should waste no time on departure. There is a jingling of the brass bell, the 5½-foot drivewheels spin, and plumes of grayish smoke mushroom high from the accelerating engine.

Here is Plymouth, a fast-growing village. A new bank has just been formed in this shire town, one of three court centers in Grafton County. Daniel Webster once practiced here. There is normally a noonday dinner stop for half an hour; today, our stop will be longer. The delay is occasioned by the "up" freight, 25 empty platform cars and five boxcars, which got stalled down the line. *Granite State* and *Winnipiseogie* on the front finally heave in sight on their way to Warren. BC&M platform cars have no brakes of any kind, so (if available) there are usually some boxcars added for braking power. The rear car is a BC&M "freight saloon," a side-door caboose built from a former boxcar with room provided for freight packages, one or two passengers and the crew. Because of the Lake Village roundhouse fire, motive power is short, so these engines will make two round trips before an exhausting day is over. To our right is the old Pemigewasset stagecoach hotel now enjoying a boom thanks to the railroad. Plymouth is beginning to receive a modest summer patronage from visitors to the White Mountains. The stagecoaches follow gravel roads up along the Pemigewasset River past the Flume to Franconia Notch. From there travelers stage northward via Franconia Village to Littleton, thence by White Mountains RR to Woodsville. We admire the main office of the BC&M, a pleasant Grecian-style structure a few rods from the hotel. Mr. Whiton, superintendent, and Mr. Dodge, freight agent, swing aboard for Concord.

We follow the Pemigewasset River for a few miles, and then strike

"Winnipeseogie" poses at the new Fabyan House in 1877. *Walker Collection*

through the fields and woods to cross the 678-foot summit of Fogg's Hill. Fogg's has a 1½% grade on both sides, so the fireman fills the firebox full of wood, which sputters and gradually adds enough energy to maintain a pressure of 125 pounds. The plunger pumps are turned off until after the summit.

We reach the top, proceeding carefully and slowly, rather than blasting up and over. The puffing quiets down, and by now our brakeman has tightened brakes on the first coach, enough to hold the train as we drift downgrade to Meredith Village, an important town with inns and a busy stagecoach connection with Sandwich, Wolfborough and the eastern towns of Carroll County. The turntable and small engine house are useful for

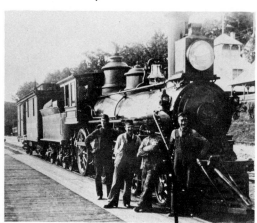

BC&M "Coos," built by Manchester for passenger service, shown here at Weirs with "freight saloon," or sidedoor caboose. *Smithsonian*

helper engines. Rounding a long curve near Meredith Depot, Lake Winnipiseogie, or Winnipesaukee, that vast sheet of water lies before us, 22 miles
long, with 300 islands, so they say, and views of the Belknap and Ossipee
Ranges. Our train is nearly half full, a few more than the usual 50 or 60
passengers per train. We leave Meredith, following the lake shore. One
reflects on how often the builders surveyed along the banks of lakes or
rivers because these provided the easiest route.

Bounding along over the precarious English iron rails, we pass the
steamboat terminal at Weirs, named for the fish nets once placed there by
Indians. We glimpse BC&M's great 125-foot paddle-wheel steamer, *Lady
of the Lake,* docked for the winter. She has been well-patronized and
profitable every summer since purchase in 1852. Next spring Captain
Walker resumes his regular route: Weirs to Senter's Hotel at Centre
Harbor, then down lake to Wolfborough.

Our little train puffs and shrieks around a point of land to Paugus Bay.
The long trestle here is the scene of BC&M's worst tragedy. After the
State Agricultural Fair in 1854 at Laconia, the BC&M *Special* was proceeding northbound to Meredith and Plymouth. A dozen young fellows
jumped on the engine's front running boards, hoping to escape payment
of trainfare. The conductor that day was not about to allow free riding.

14

Facing page: **Graceful excursion steamer, "Lady of the Lake."** *Dick Learned*

Below: **Boston, Concord & Montreal mainline crosses Paugus Bay of Lake Winnipesaukee near present-day Lakeport. Steamer "James Bell" tied up at the railroad dock.** *Laconia Library*

He stopped the train on the wooden trestle, walked forward, and was collecting cash for fares. Without warning the regular "up" passenger train burst around a curve and plunged headlong into the stopped special. Six persons were killed outright, 40 badly hurt. It was a day of tragedies. Earlier, a woman had caught her foot in the track at Meredith Bridge and was killed when an engine, unable to stop in time, came churning up the track.

Just beyond the trestle where BC&M crosses from west to east of the Winnipesaukee River, were the main shops of the railroad, now charred ruins. Six days past, during a snowy, cold, windy night, both shop and engine house took fire. Mr. Stevens, master of machinery, is assessing the damage, and will report to Mr. Quincy today. The newspapers already set the loss at $60,000. There were four engines in the fire. *Pehaungun,* a freight engine, can run again, as well as *Moosilauk* and *Old Man of the Mountains,* the historic engine that pulled the first BC&M train in 1848. Worst of all, the seven-year-old *Josiah Quincy,* named after the president, has been seriously damaged. Only just repaired with a new firebox and other improvements, it may never run again. It will probably be pushed out north of the ruined engine house and used as a source of parts. There is talk of building an engine house in Concord. Fortunately, BC&M has

15

several acres which could be used for that purpose but, with money scarce, it seems better to share Northern RR's brick roundhouse, and rebuild the shop gradually.

Near Lake Village our train comes to Laconia, "set off" from Gilford in 1855 as an independent town. A strong volume of water power offers promise to industry. Passing south of the river, shiny *Elkins* rolls along the shores of Winnisquam Lake, and at Lochmere we again cross the waters. Silver Lake glints in the pale winter sunlight. No wonder the directors were able to "congratulate" the stockholders. Except for the long cut at Warren Summit, most of the BC&M roadbed was just a matter of rearranging gravel. The engineers had estimated a cost of $109,000 per mile, but by thrift and good fortune the original 18 miles of line from Concord cost only $53,000 per mile. At any higher figure, it could not have been built so far as Plymouth. Boston financiers had never warmed up to BC&M; they were occupied with the burgeoning West, not to mention profitable factories right in Massachusetts. Why take on the uncertainties of a country railroad in the icy forests of New Hampshire? The line had to be financed locally, even, so it was said, "with earnings of millgirls."

Rolling and pitching, *Elkins* steams bravely on, crossing the Winnisquam River not far from the long engine house which served BC&M when it built its first 18 miles to Sanbornton Bridge. A long whistle for the crossing. Sparks spring high into the air as *Elkins* clatters down the uncertain way. Normally, we stop at Northfield Station, with its two enormous woodsheds, to take on enough fuel for Concord and return. An old horse tramps endless miles on a treadmill which powers the cutoff saw. Wood is scarce in this area and must be brought down from distant farms. Except for a few apple trees the landscape is nearly bare; here and there clumps of sun-loving pine trees commence to grow among the stumps.

We enter the flood plain of the Merrimac River, where the grade is fairly level, as we prepare to stop at Canterbury. A few prosperous stockholders will get on at Canterbury, but no one at all from the busy Shaker settlement a few miles to the east. Nearly 300 members work at producing farm and light manufactured products, but not a Shaker soul leaves for such a worldly purpose as doctoring an ailing young railroad. The sidetracks are full of loaded cars, mostly hardware, dry goods, and foodstuffs coming to the local merchants. A passenger engine, *Ahquedauken,* puffs silently on a sidetrack ready to back out, after we pass by, to pull its dozen loads of boxcars and empty cattlecars up the line. Stock cars on the BC&M are boxcars with slatted doors; there is a sizeable traffic in steers and horses bound from Haverhill to the Cambridge markets. Freight engines and crews normally work all the way to Boston and back.

Last stop is the pleasant village of East Concord. With our train nearly filled, we cross the Merrimack on a creaking, groaning, three-arch covered bridge, drifting with throttle off and dampers closed so as not to set fire to the bridge. On the distant horizon is the glinting capital dome at Concord.

Our engineer turns his plunger pumps full on. As we near the big station, it will be important to have a filled boiler after we come to a halt. Five other roads use the two-track depot building, and trains are forever running in and out to load and unload. The *Elkins* comes to a stop amidst the hub-bub, and already our confidence is restored. Surely there must be enough wealth down country to help the up-country line!

Top photo: Wavy roof line and broken windows of BC&M wheel shop at Lake Village, N. H., only faintly disguise favorite Greek revival architecture. Store in background is the only building in this rare photo which still exists. *Bottom photo:* No, the Lake Village shops are not on fire this time. Concord & Montreal 4—4—0 gets up steam as 0—4—0 "Paugus" switches the yard. *Laconia Library*

This portrait, warts and all, of Josiah Quincy hangs today in the State House at Concord. *Bill Finney photo*

The notion of building a Boston, Concord & Montreal RR had been boldly conceived during the early 1840's, soon after the Concord RR had been built into the state capital in 1842. The BC&M plan was to follow a pioneer stagecoach route north along the New Hampshire lakes, thence to Plymouth, Haverhill, and a connection for Canada at Wells River, Vt. The Connecticut & Passumpsic Rivers RR, building north from White River Junction to Wells River, had been warmly receptive to BC&M plans —at first. C&P would ostensibly gain from a BC&M source of traffic exchange. To frost that particular cake, a plan arose to link Meredith on the BC&M with the seacoast via a north shore railroad along Lake Winnipesaukee, but this plan never materialized. By adroit maneuvering under the wily generalship of Judge George W. Nesmith, the Northern RR (see map) bribed the C&P with a convenient loan; so that C&P reneged on its promise to form an interchange at Wells River.

Thus thwarted, BC&M's next hope was to seek control of the broken-down White Mountains RR and extend it north from Littleton toward the Canadian border, perhaps intersecting the new Atlantic & St. Lawrence at Northumberland. The A&SL, built by British interests, connected Montreal with Portland, Maine. Yet another possible connection remained. There was a Montpelier & Wells River* RR planned from Montpelier, the Vermont capital, east to Wells River but, partly because of severe grades and sparse territory, it never became an important trunk line.

The New Hampshire deadlock was finally broken in 1844. Persons of the stature of Dartmouth College Professor Charles B. Haddock argued forcefully and persuasively on behalf of railroads, pointing out that land values and farm prices would increase, while travel would be more convenient, if only the necessary railroads could be built. With the wisdom of compromise the balky New Hampshire General Court chartered not one but five railroads in 1844, among them the Boston, Concord & Montreal.

* Originally Montpelier & Connecticut River.

The organization and first construction of the BC&M proceeded apace. Incorporated on December 27, 1844, its first meeting was held on April 8, 1845, and its by-laws adopted on October 30. The directors planned first to build to Plymouth, N.H. and to purchase four engines, six passenger coaches, three baggage cars, and 50 freight cars. To save money, they planned to use 42-pound iron rail using many sleepers instead of 56-pound on fewer sleepers. (Eventually they compromised, choosing 50-pound rail.) Among the early "road furniture" were 16 low-cost, four-wheel box and platform cars, another example of New England economy. With ten years to go on their charter, the directors hurried to raise what funds they could from the sale of capital stock.

The ceremonial "first shovelful" was turned with appropriate fanfare and speechmaking on February 7, 1846. Though it was reported that "throughout the whole route, the most friendly feeling toward the road exists . . ." the treasurer did have to mention that ". . . the stockholders in our road are nearly all residents in the country, and assessments are not usually available from them with that nice punctuality that attends subscriptions in the city." Was it cold feet or second guessing that caused such reluctance? It was, the directors opined, "a period of severe embarrassment in the affairs of the community . . . Money has been scarce . . . There is a deranged condition of things abroad."

Thanks, however, to easy grading conditions, construction moved rapidly for the first 18 miles from Concord to Sanbornton Bridge (now Tilton). *Old Man of the Mountains,* a high-wheel woodburning 4—4—0 made the first run on May 22, 1848, with its train painted from cowcatcher to rear coach in brilliant sky blue. Perhaps the directors were having their own private joke about fanciful financial schemes known even today as "blue sky." A few days later, June 1st welcomed the first regular freight train. Freight engines were heavier and equipped with smaller drivewheels than passenger engines, but in respects such as paint and brasswork were no less glorious. As a traveler of the day remarked, the weather might be so cold that all seats near the center stove were taken and the sperm oil lamps on the ends of the car so feeble that one could not even see how many passengers there were in the car, but he could ride assured that the engine up ahead was painted and well-polished. By this time the road had cost $215,176.11. Now it was a matter of finding a dollar to pay for each rail. (A second helping of capital in 1854 would be called, in fact, the "Iron Stock.")

When a train under Conductor Major "Jake" Libby reached Meredith Bridge, now Laconia, on August 8, 1848, great was the exultation. In answer to the locomotive whistle, cannon were fired, then mill bells picked up the signal, to be followed by all the church bells within hearing.

"The work has progressed steadily, if not quite as rapidly as might be wished," rambled one of the frequent official messages of encouragement. The inexpensive roadbed was pushed well ahead of rail, but it was not until January 21, 1850, that the track at last reached Plymouth. Established stagecoach interests had, of course, not been idle; they always did their best to discourage railroads north of Concord. Now a new rivalry arose. Northern RR built a branch up the Pemigewasset to Bristol in 1848, with stage connections to Plymouth. BC&M countered by subsidizing a rival stageline. This "Stage War" cost BC&M $8,000, in those days a princely amount.

Year 1848 saw the road surveyed to West Rumney and a locomotive roster of three 18-ton passenger and two 20-ton freight engines. The sum of $969,686 had been expended, $759,460 of it from the sale of stock and $127,851 from notes and bonds. The difference of approximately $84,000 was made up out of operating profits. BC&M had created its own treadmill. Trains made profits to pay for construction to extend the line in order to realize the hopes and aspirations of its note and stockholders. Where would it end?

By 1850, slightly over $1 million of capital stock had been sold. There were also $82,00) of bonds and $203,000 of short term "floating" debt. Could BC&M feel opt mistic? There was Concord RR paying 10% dividends on a busy double track line from Boston clear to Concord. Deposits flowered among 35 banks. Cotton and woolen manufacturing and livestock raising, not to mention butter, cheese, and maple syrup, were flourishing enterprises. Furthermore, New Hampshire population expanded by 75% between 1800 and 1850. Signs of progress were statewide.

BC&M pushed forward to Warren; the operating report of 1851 showed passenger revenues of $70,755; freight, $69,949; mail, $2,793; miscellaneous, $1,737. But operating expense included track rental fees to the "lower

For the photographer's benefit, the train crew decorated the "Crawford" prior to another death-defying run over the uncertain rails. *Ry. & Locomotive Hist. Soc.*

Two unidentified early BC&M engines, possibly "Granite State" and "McDuffie," pose atop the Woodsville-Wells River bridge. Lower section was a toll bridge for for horse-drawn traffic. *Walker Collection*

roads," including rich Concord RR, of $43,576, equal to 30% of revenues, and almost as high as the road's own expenses of $52,672. Gross operating profit of $48,676 was almost entirely eroded away by interest and amortization payments. Not only did BC&M pay a substantial ransom to the greedy lower roads, but had to contend with snow, ice, and other problems of wilderness railroading.

BC&M issued new 6% preferred stock in 1852. Stockholders bought $200,000 worth. Contractors were obliged to accept another $200,000. The steam-power press of printers McFarland & Jenks spewed forth BC&M paper certificates.

Remember that BC&M's original plan was to cross the Connecticut River at Wells River, Vermont, and that the Connecticut & Passumpsic RR, determined to hinder the rural upstart, obtained a loan and side-stepped a commitment. Not to be outfoxed, BC&M selected an alternative site *two* miles south of the Vermont town and there built a bridge. The C&P counterpunched with a force of men who put "dirt and other obstructions" in the way. The president of C&P was then also the Governor of Vermont. Having, as it is said, the legislature "in his pocket," no relief was forthcoming from that source. For a second time the C&P men came and mussed up BC&M's graded road bed, but BC&M brought in a superior force, drove off the Passumpsic men, and got the project back on schedule. The C&P backed down. A two-story deck-bridge was built at Wells River, for $20,000, operated by the BC&M-owned Wells River Bridge Co. The lower deck was a toll bridge for highway traffic. "The great enterprise is completed," trumpeted the directors' report: "A great line of road, the largest in the state." With 93 miles of track, it was at least the *longest*. The first BC&M train steamed into Wells River on May 10, 1853.

On July 1, BC&M extended its reach another 20 miles by leasing the White Mountains RR. This local affair had been incorporated on December 25, 1848, and chartered to build to Lancaster. Ira Goodall of Bath (N.H.) was president. The first train, Wells River to Littleton, ran on August 1, 1853.

Counting on a five-year agreement with the Connecticut & Passumpsic to send half its traffic via BC&M and half by Northern RR, BC&M increased its rates, continued ballasting, bought real estate, built stations, added shop buildings, and rounded out its rolling stock. The repair shop built at Lake Village, was "a most convenient point and affording all the facilities and conveniences for keeping our machinery in a most effective state." Now there were 14 engines, most of them built by Hinkley in Boston. Four passenger trains a day plus freights were the rule. Mr. Elkins, BC&M's manager, passed away that year. He was replaced by James M.

Venerable "Peter Clark," with wooden cab, lengthlong running boards and typical Boston, Concord & Montreal early smokestack, hauled freight and work trains for many years up the Mountain Road to Littleton and beyond. *Railway & Locomotive Historical Society*

Whiton, formerly of the Concord RR. Among the problems Mr. Whiton faced was the replacement of 17,000 sleepers—every year!—and the hardening of 400 tons of soft Welsh rail into tougher "Swede's Iron." This had to be accomplished by arduous labor over a forge and anvil by blacksmiths. The Woodsville car house was destroyed by a wind storm and, to top it off, every year two or three drunks "full of bad liquor" fell afoul of moving trains at one place or another along the way. To occupy idle moments, there was a $50,000 lawsuit with contractor Warren Smith. The job paid Whiton $2,000 annually, pretty fair by BC&M standards.

Thus, during the harsh winter of 1857, BC&M stockholders were probably not overly surprised to learn from their January newspapers that a special meeting would be held at Depot Hall, Concord, on February 5th, "to provide ways and means to pay the debt of the corporation." According to the press, "the meeting was very fully attended." Our fellow passenger, Josiah Quincy, "in a speech of considerable length," asserted that assets were worth $2 million. But, despite a debt of only $1 million, there remained an embarrassing unsecured, or "floating," debt of $230,000.

The long and short of the meeting was that approval was given to exchange medium term bonds for floating notes and that a stockholders' committee would investigate the affairs of the company, and report back in 30 days.

This "Minot Committee" was composed of prominent gentlemen from Haverhill, Laconia, and Sanbornton and also, peradventure, one Joseph A. Gilmore of Concord, later to be exposed as a notorious rascal of the Concord RR. (The committee absented itself for only 30 minutes. During this time a Mr. Buck of Haverhill introduced a motion to "restrain free riding" over the BC&M on the grounds that "this corporation is in debt and needs every dollar the road can earn." Amid considerable jollity, the motion was passed.)

Reduced to a committee of five—without Mr. Gilmore!—the Minot Committee of Investigation then made a remarkably detailed audit of the property, in reality an inventory of a typical pre-Civil War railroad down to the last spike. They found fault with the BC&M woodcutting operation at Warren, concluding it would be cheaper to purchase wood from contractors. They discovered that the directors had arranged a cozy rigging system for the stock and bond prices in Boston. (A friendly broker agreed to purchase small quantities of BC&M securities at artificial prices, thereby sustaining the market. He was in turn reimbursed by the railroad.) The committee stated its suspicion that certain employees were also suppliers of materials, not necessarily at the lowest prices. Nevertheless, they found the railroad in reasonable physical condition and capable of producing a yearly profit of $120,000. They recommended that the creditors take income bonds. Interest charges would be equal to half estimated net; the balance was allotted to sinking funds to retire the bonds.

Scarcely a detail was omitted. The Committee's report even showed that Mr. Timothy Foley received $1.00 per day as a passenger car cleaner. This being well before the days of Women's Liberation, Mrs. Foley, who also cleaned cars, received but 50 cents for the same work.

The inventory listed six small snowplows of the kind that bolt to the ends of flat cars. There were also three large "snow gougers," one of them called *Cyclone*. Everything on the BC&M had a name, even snowplows.

The report was filed in March, but creditors fudged about accepting the new bonds. To shake the money tree, the directors planted ads in the papers setting dates for stockholder meetings to discuss the outright sale of BC&M at auction. Meanwhile, White Mountains RR announced insolvency, followed by the Contoocook Valley and the Portsmouth & Concord. Fares were reduced; Concord RR cut back train schedules. The firm of Jay Cooke & Co. failed; and the Panic of 1857 consumed dozens of railroads and put hundreds of companies in bankruptcy. Most of the BC&M board resigned, leaving only Quincy and Coffin of the previous group. Apparently, however, BC&M was able to exert "rigid economy" and thus pacify short-term creditors. The company remained technically solvent. Train service continued—by a miracle.

By 1859, the directors declared "a brighter day is dawning." Profits hovered in the $90,000 range, and $274,000 of notes had been refinanced, half from stockholder new money and half by the issuance of new 6% sinking fund mortgage bonds to creditors.

1864 service report: George W. Stevens, fireman, worked on "James N. Elkins," "McDuffie," "Pehaungun" and "Ahquedauken" during the month of March. He was paid the grand total of $11.25 for fifteen days of effort. *Doran Jones*

The second Pemmigewasset House at Plymouth was built in 1864, served quick dinners to tired passengers on the BC&M. A celebrated visitor, writer Nathaniel Hawthorne, passed away here in 1864. *Doran Jones*

III

Its financial crunch postponed, BC&M returned to workaday problems that historian Alvin Harlow termed a "lone-hand fight for life," for not till 1864 did traffic turn upward. BC&M's secret ally was water power from lakes and rivers. Largely with the help of Massachusetts money, factories were constructed for the output of ready made clothing, first for soldiers, afterward for general public consumption. Typical "Mill Streets" in New Hampshire began to produce knitted stockings, footwear, trousers, gloves, towels and textile machinery. Families such as the Busiels, Tiltons and Sulloways achieved prominence. Sleepy villages became, almost overnight, big producers of freight tonnage. By 1868, BC&M profits blossomed to $150,948, of which $137,500 was soaked up by interest, sinking funds, and preferred dividends. Notwithstanding that ordinary stockholders had received no cash in 20 years (only scrip or stock dividends) the directors resumed talk about extension northward in accord with the road's original ambitions.

The first extension was completed from Littleton to Lancaster on October 31, 1870, using old 50-pound iron from the main line, itself relaid with new 56-pound steel rails. There were three new engines, including *Franconia* from the famous ship-turned-engine-builder, McKay & Aldus. Two years later tracks were extended to the Grand Trunk Ry. (formerly Atlantic & St. Lawrence) at Groveton in the town of Northumberland.

Nagging problems remained: BC&M, blaming "not so favorable" contracts, was still shelling out nearly a third of revenues to the insatiable lower roads. Also, it was quicker and cheaper to ship and travel via Northern RR and Connecticut & Passumpsic. Despite traffic agreements, BC&M lost volume. For example, a passenger from Wells River paid $3.50 to take the BC&M 9:10 train to arrive at Concord at 3:28 (assuming it was on time). For only five cents more, the 10:35 C&P from Wells River would reach Concord at 3:25. Rival Northern RR was using big Moguls over its comparatively smooth and level track; maximum grade was 60 feet to the mile, compared to 90 feet on the BC&M. One way or another, BC&M was being badly squeezed.

Pecuniary lapses were frequent. In 1870, the BC&M treasurer forgot or failed to pay the town tax in Warren. One day, the engine of the "down" passenger train was attached by the Sheriff, and it could not move until the treasurer himself was contacted by telegraph.

In July, 1869, the Mt. Washington cog railroad opened for service, with a BC&M 25% financial interest from the start. Its strange 6-ton cogwheel engines clattered up and down the steeply graded 3.17 miles of track laid to the odd gauge of 4 feet, 7½ inches. When President of the United States General U. S. Grant came to see the line, his private party traveled over BC&M as far as Twin Mountain, thence to Base Station by horse and wagon. Grant's special sleeping car attracted attention—a conspicuous harbinger of things to come. For the notion of the summer vacation was dawning on New Englanders, rich from the post-Civil War boom. Soon Old Crawford's family inns at the Notch were supplemented by dozens of large and small hotels as the trickle of pioneer mountain explorers ripened into a stream of comfort-seeking nabobs and their families.

On July 4, 1874, track was finished from Wing Road through Twin Mountain to Fabyans. After the little White Mountains RR lease ran out, the road was purchased in 1873 for $300,000 in BC&M bonds; for a few years BC&M ostentatiously called itself the "Boston, Concord, Montreal, White Mountains and Mt. Washington Branch Railroads." Now there were 26 steam engines, 23 coaches, 13 baggage cars and 595 freight cars. The Lake Village shops and engine house had finally been rebuilt after the galling 1857 disaster. Freight tonnage, meanwhile, was twice pre-Civil War volume. Revenues totaled $664,197 and profits $140,208, but the operating ratio was nearly 80%, rather too high for comfort.

A new logging railroad from Whitefield to Jefferson Highlands, was chartered on July 11, 1878, by Brown Lumbering Co. It tapped the lush forests north of the Presidential Range, and was probably one of the first out-and-out lumbering railroads in the United States. This Whitefield & Jefferson RR eventually operated four engines, including the *Starr King* and *Waumbek*. BC&M leased the road in 1879, and brought in passenger trains to the plush Waumbek House at Jefferson.

Extensions of the BC&M were in reality logging railroads. The road literally financed its progress by hauling timber. To carry outsize logs, BC&M men took trucks from scrapped freight cars. Logs were loaded on the trucks and, fastened by chains, themselves constituted the car frame; whole forests thus rolled off to the mills. Nearly 20 miles of sidetracks were almost entirely devoted at this time to the loading of logs and lumber, and thousands of acres were made barren to satisfy the housing needs of an

Mt. Washington Railway, A BC&M affiliate, bought cog engine No. 6 in 1874, same year BC&M tracks reached Base Station. With typical BC&M smokestack, No. 6 was last of the vertical-boilered cog engines, first with four cylinders.
Edgar T. Mead

expanding urban population. Softwood went for lumber, hardwood for furniture or manufactured articles such as bobbins and shoetrees.

The 14-mile Kilkenny Lumber RR ran from Lancaster eastward into the forests *via* Whipple's Mill and Webster's to Kilkenny near Mt. Cabot. The branch became a useful dumping point for outworn rail and motive power. Still another lumber branch was the 7-mile Zealand Valley RR built in 1883 by the assertive Henry interests, from near Twin Mountain south along the Zealand River to Ethan's Pond. Its premier motive power was an antique 0—4—0 built in '39 for Massachusetts' Western RR. The second was a 25-ton Baldwin 1886 saddleback named *Tintah*.

On March 1, 1883, the first train from Plymouth puffed into North Woodstock over the 20-mile Pemigewasset Valley RR. From the start,

"Starr King," veteran of the rough Whitefield & Jefferson log road, finally gave up at Belmont while on easy branchline duties.
Doran Jones

BC&M's intention was to assist in construction and to lease the PV for operations. Two engines, *Campton* and *Thornton,* were assigned but not restricted to the branch. Directly above North Woodstock depot was the Deer Park Hotel, a popular jumping-off spot for the Flume. A one-mile "Lincoln Extension" was built in 1892 when railroad logging began in earnest on the forest fastness of the Pemigewasset River East Branch.

Year 1874 saw BC&M purchase the first of its luxury coaches, variously known as parlor, boudoir, or drawing room cars. These boasted an exotic hardwood interior, fancy silvered oil lamps, wide windows, and comfortable plush armchairs. Anticipating slow-motion train travel over bumpy track, an extra $2.00 to ride the brand-new *Plymouth* from Concord to the White Mountains must have seemed almost an expenditure of necessity to vacationing manufacturers and merchants.

Against a typical rainy, cloudy White Mountain backdrop, BC&M "Belknap" shifts lumber in a ritual BC&M activity. *Ry. & Locomotive Historical Society*

Hotel Waumbek, the Twin Mountain House, Sinclair's, Sunset Hill House, Mountain View House, and Mt. Pleasant House—to name a few— opened their doors to compete with older, illustrious establishments, such as the 1859 Crawford House.

Nor was BC&M itself dormant to the profit possibilities of hotel operation. The first venture was a rebuilt Pemigewasset House at Plymouth, destroyed in an 1863 fire. This time, it was built right next to the tracks. During half-hour meal stops, passengers could bolt a frenetic lunch on the lower floor, or stampede up a palatial staircase to the main dining room. The favorite dish was chicken potpie, kept warm if trains were late. North and southbound trains usually met at Plymouth.

To bolster its stake in the cog railway, BC&M financed the Summit House atop Mt. Washington in 1872. Travelers could spend the night to

Lumber, clapboards and shingles for BC&M's Summit House were all transported via the Mt. Washington cog line. *Edgar T. Mead*

savor the breaking of dawn venturing forth over the distant coast of Maine. Every ounce of construction material for the Summit House was hauled up over the cog line from the BC&M connection.

A third venture was the Fabyan House in 1876, built just south of the tracks at Fabyans. Though of rather plain architecture, it afforded rooms for 150 guests. Contrary to advertisements which offered the guest rest and repose, the smell of the wood and later coalburners, plus the daylong din of whistles, bells and switching operations must have created a contrary ambiance. North from Fabyans (altitude 1571 feet), BC&M built a six-mile branch along the south bank of the upper Ammonosuc River to Base Station (altitude 2668 feet): Marshfield, as it was also called. Passengers walked across a wooden platform to catch the cog trains, four or five of which would be on hand to start puffing up the mountain as soon as loaded. The connecting branch required a ruling grade of 6%, and for

A justly celebrated BC&M engine was heavy Mogul 2—6—0 "Mt. Washington," built 1876 by Manchester Works, which thereafter heaved passenger trains up the steep Fabyans-Base Station branch in summer, worked on log trains in winter. *Doran Jones*

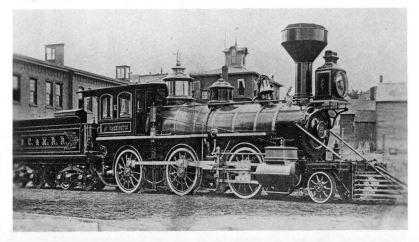

Mt. Pleasant House was bordered by Maine Central tracks from Crawford's to the south, on the north by BC&M, between Fabyans and Base Station. Cog Ry. climbs Mt. Washington just right of tree in center of this view. *Dartmouth Baker Library*

this, in June 1876, Manchester delivered what was said to be the most powerful engine in New England, the 30-ton Mogul 2—6—0 *Mt. Washington*, taking the name of an early BC&M eight-wheeler thereafter named *Carroll*. The engine always backed its train of open observation cars to Base Station. Standard Boston & Maine Moguls later took over the branch chore; the last steam engine over the line was B&M 4—4—0 905, formerly the 494, now preserved at White River Junction, Vermont.

In 1878, BC&M president John E. Lyon passed away as the result of burns suffered during a minor conflagration in his room at the Pemigewasset House. During his 18-year tenure, BC&M took over White Mountains RR and built that part of the system from Littleton to Groveton and Fabyans. His plan to build to Colebrook failed when Maine Central got there first, but he managed a successful joint traffic deal with the Maine Central-Montpelier & Wells River-St. Johnsbury & Lake Champlain system permitting interchange north, east and west. Lyon's successor was J. Thomas Vose, a board member from Boston.

Poets and artists had for years pictured the beauties of Franconia Notch, among them Whittier, Longfellow, Edward Everett, Emerson and Hawthorne, whose *Great Stone Face* story referred to the famous "Profile." Thus, Echo Lake, Profile Lake, and the "Old Man of the Mountains" were entirely familiar to eastern city dwellers. Presidents, congressmen, diplomats and foreign visitors came and went, their visits heralded in the metropolitan papers. Higher altitude towns, such as Bethlehem and Jefferson, were merchandised as relief for hay fever sufferers. Add to this a profusion of resort literature, most of it issued by the railroads. Lavish prose encouraged vacations in the White Mountains and, predictably, hordes descended on the frail ecology as soon as "winter unlock'd its icy grasp." The poets, artists and hikers might stay at farm and rooming houses, but the newly rich sought out what were currently among the most expensive lodgings in the United States, notably the Profile House at Franconia Notch.

At first, travelers wishing to see the Notch and the famous Flume took the train to Plymouth and changed over to a fatiguing stagecoach ride. Accordingly, the proprietors of the Profile House, Taft and Greenleaf, joined BC&M in incorporating a ten-mile railroad branching from near Bethlehem Junction to a depot just east of their splendid hotel. Completed on June 25, 1879, the Profile & Franconia Notch RR used a track gauge of three feet. The engines burned wood, were 4—4—0 types, and—in the BC&M manner—carried names, in this case *Profile* and *Echo*. There were originally two coaches, two combination cars, six freight cars and a two-track engine house at Bethlehem. The road was surveyed to Flume House, but never got there, though a 3.38 mile branch was put into Bethlehem

Guests reached Mr. Greenleaf's splendidly sophisticated Profile House by steam narrow-gauge railway *(below)*, whose station shows faintly through the trees at lower right. Building still exists as a gift shop. *From Learned and Dartmouth Col.*

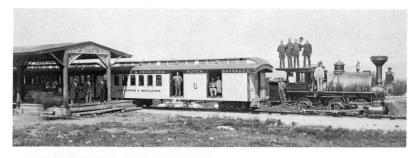

Annual passes from BC&M's narrow-gauge affiliate were a useful as well as ornamental keepsake. There's no record whether Mr. Kingsbury of Cheshire & Monadnock RR ever took up Mr. Greenleaf's cordial invitation. *Walter Wright*

Signs of feverish construction adorn the brand-new Fabyans Station and the Fabyan House around 1875. *Doran Jones*

Street in July, 1881, powered by a comical o—6—o saddletank which backed its cars to Maplewood and Bethlehem. Trains shuttled back and forth all day long.

Travelers from New York were blandished to visit the mountains *via* Long Island Sound steamers to New London, Conn., or Fall River, Mass., where direct train connections were maintained for Concord. BC&M and Norwich & Worcester RR parlor cars were exchanged for a while. BC&M proudly advertised that it used "monitor" roof coaches. Later on, the Ranlet Laconia Car Co. an on-line industry, supplied cars with the latest "French Top." Both the monitor and French Top roofs provided a row of ventilators for air circulation and glass panels for light, instead of the flat or curved roofs used on the earliest coaches.

Perched atop the double-decked Woodsville-Wells River bridge is an 1870 vintage BC&M train with "French Top" baggage car and the latest thing in monitor roofs for the coaches. Rear car advertises Lake Winnipesaukee, Plymouth and Littleton on its letterboards. *Railway & Locomotive Historical Society, also Rail Photo Service*

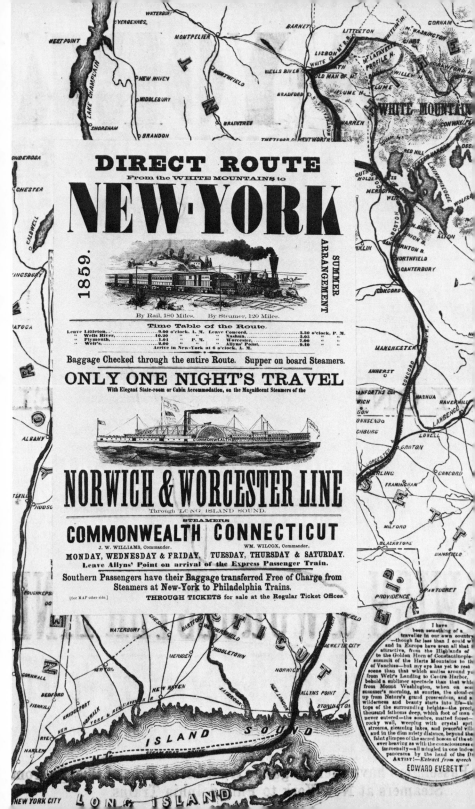

Through the entire decade of the 1870's, BC&M remained steadfastly a wood-burning railroad. Each year about 30,000 cords of wood were consumed at average cost of $2.50 per cord, a total of $75,000, equal to nearly 11% of revenues. As long ago as 1858, the Boston & Lowell converted to coal, with savings of one-third. Why was BC&M committed to wood? First and obviously, wood was plentiful; second, the lower roads soaked high tariffs for shipping coal. Third, BC&M engines, being designed for wood, tended to constipate themselves whenever coal was tried.

Passenger trains were equipped with air brakes starting in 1872, when the pride of the fleet, *Chocorua,* was modernized. Freight trains still relied on hand brakes. When the engineer whistled "down brakes," out came the crew from their side-door "freight saloon" caboose to tighten the brakewheels.

Operating chief of the BC&M at Plymouth for the years 1849–1883 was Joseph A. Dodge, recalled as a brusque and imperious gentleman. His successor some years later was George E. Cummings, who worked from 1868 to 1919, a total of 55 years. Cummings started as watchman and engine cleaner, was at various time brakeman, shopman, wood-purchasing agent, freight-transfer agent, train-master, superintendent of the Kilkenny RR, assistant superintendent, and finally superintendent of lines north of Concord. Another memorable BC&M superintendent was Edward F. Mann of Woodsville.

Winter operation required man-sized exertion. George G. Hutchins, engineer, ran a plow train for six days and six nights on one occasion during 1870 with only six hours of sleep. His paycheck was $24. The wood burners weren't much good in wet snow; they derailed with ease if ice was not removed from crossings and switches.

ior to the War of the Rebellion, the correct way to the White Mountains volved a comfortable overnight voyage from New York City to Norwich, Conn., ence by rail north to Plymouth, N. H., and a civilized coach ride on to ttleton and beyond. Paean of praise *(circle inset)* for New Hampshire ountains and lakes is by Edward Everett, co-speaker with Abraham Lincoln Gettysburg. *Dartmouth College*

Above: Local firemen trudge past BC&M Lake Village shops, trainload of logs, and tiny Greek revival station, watching carefully for horse leavings and rails of the Laconia Street Railway. *Below:* BC&M passenger car shop at left was removed when Lake Shore Branch to Alton Bay was built. Present-day view is almost totally different: new buildings, tall trees and a wide concrete highway. *Laconia Library*

THE YEAR 1882 WAS FATEFUL FOR WRECKS. Newsman C. E. Caswell tells how in May 22 loaded cars broke loose at North Haverhill and rolled downhill straight into the local way freight: "Conductor George Stone and his brakeman were in the caboose asleep. The way freight crew heard the cars coming down through the woods opposite the Keyes farm and could have saved themselves, but the crash came, and thirty seconds later there was the greatest pile of junk the road had ever seen. The *Granite State,* in charge of Engineer Whiting was hauling the way freight. She was hurled completely over a fence, bottom side up, with the dead body of Conductor Stone from the smashed caboose crushed between the steam dome and the sand box. He was killed instantly, as was the brakeman, who was found in a boxcar of the way freight two cars back. He was thrown from inside their buggy, over the way freight engine, and into a wrecked car, so great was the impact. Arthur Knapp was waiting for the way freight when the loose cars passed through, and said they were certainly going 70 miles per hour. He said in three minutes he heard the collision distinctly in the morning air, four miles away. The way freight crew as a whole had a narrow escape, and a fireman by the name of Fellows was so badly frightened, he resigned when he arrived at the terminal."

That Fall the *Plymouth* with a mail train of four cars left Concord at 3:10 P.M. as usual and proceeded north to Tilton, receiving orders to meet the "down" cattle train at Meredith Village. *Plymouth* backed on to a siding to await the cattle train, but new orders instructed the mail train to meet both the cattle train and the "down" express at Plymouth. About halfway between Ashland and Plymouth, engineer Peebles of the mail train saw the cattle train rounding the curve. He hit the air brakes. So did engineer Quimby aboard *Franconia.* Most of the crews jumped, and seconds later the two engines smashed into each other. *Franconia* was turned nearly three-fourths of the way around to the north, *Plymouth*

"Plymouth" and "Franconia" tangle at Long Pond on Ashland Hill. *Doran Jones*

partly around to the south. The two tenders were thrown to the east side of the track, and the baggage car splintered to kindling wood. Some cattle cars full of horses were thrown off on the opposite side from the engines. Two passengers, one a drover, were killed.

On a road so empty of safety standards, it is amazing more accidents did not occur.

In 1878, Conductor Wyatt fell to his death between the cars. "No blame," said the annual report, "attached to the company." Frank Smith of Haverhill was knocked from the top of his train by striking a bridge at Weirs; he died in a few hours. Again, "no blame was attached to the road." In 1880, John Butler caught a foot in a guard rail and was run over. Eugene W. Ford, employed as a freight brakeman, struck his head against a bridge. Conductor L. G. Johnson was thrown from the train by the breaking of a brake chain. Again, "no blame is attached to the company." The bereaved families were scared to death of the company's attorneys, and the state authorities paid scant attention.

With the exception of *Paugus* 0—4—0 and *Mt. Washington* 2—6—0, all BC&M engines were 4—4—0's. *Canterbury* and *Wentworth,* purchased in 1883, were not dissimilar to engines obtained prior to the Civil War. No longer could the road assign one man to one engine, because crew members repeatedly "went west" to seek rich wages on the roaring roads in Colorado and California. After 1870, engines were numbered, partly to avoid confusion and partly to save time in telegraphic train orders. Older

engines were weeded out by wrecks or else downgraded into helpers or switchers, bereft of their distinctive horizontal-bar cowcatchers. With the exception of the early engines, all power was built at Manchester, N.H.

BC&M employed more than its share of characters. One of these was an eccentric fellow by the name of Joe Ayer, nicknamed "Joe Hooker" after the Civil War general. Working long hours like other BC&M men, Joe would take catnaps, head against the cab back and feet resting on the reverse lever. Somehow, he sensed the exact location of each station and crossing, awakening at any suspicion of trouble. He carried a blacksnake whip in his pocket, and as the old wood burner *Belknap* fought for each inch on the hill, he would produce the whip and flail away at the boiler.

Typical passenger trains consisted of a baggage car for mail, a baggage and Cheney's Express combine, a smoking car, and a standard passenger car. A one-car local operating between Plymouth and Concord was nicknamed the "Shoo-Fly." Passenger trains had fancy assigned names such as the *Montreal Express, Mail Train,* and so forth, but people along the way knew them by the conductor's name. A famous one was "Eastman's Train." From Woodsville, 450 feet altitude, tracks ascended to 1019 feet at Wing Road, and 1571 at Fabyans, a climb of 1121 feet in 60 miles, which freights usually double-headed. Double-heading had its advantages. On this frugal New Hampshire road, it permitted the use of light rail. Also, if one engine broke down, another remained to move its train to the nearest sidetrack.

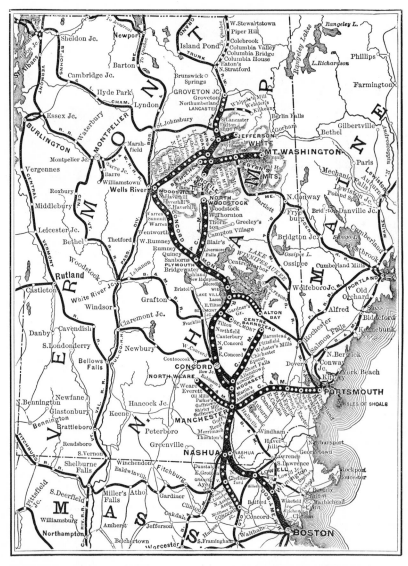

Public timetable map of 1892 shows the system just before the W&J branch was extended to Gorham and Berljn. "Like a great spider," the Concord RR was anchored on Manchester, its branches reaching out to encompass North Weare, Center Barnstead and Portsmouth. *Edgar T. Mead*

By 1883, BC&M REVENUES were up to $920,195, for a profit of $222,544 at an operating ratio of 75%. Wood fuel expenditures of $122,131 claimed 13% of revenues. The equipment roster boasted 37 engines, 21 coaches, 5 parlor and three observation cars. The road carried 343,630 passengers that year at average 3.3¢ per mile and 324,132 tons of freight at average 1.97¢ per mile.

With the haunting bond maturities of 1865 and 1875 at last paid off the way was, theoretically, free for dividends. An interim plan to consolidate the stock issues had failed because of what the directors charitably termed "reluctance." To say the least, stockholders were extremely pessimistic, as there would be no dividends anyway until bond arrearages were made good. Many old-time shareholders sold out at a loss; meanwhile, speculating millowners and city financial men bought stock during frequent roller coaster market dips. One new owner, for example, was Benjamin A. Kimball of Concord, a factory owner graduate of the railroad's mechanical department. Another was Boston financier Samuel C. Bell.

If the years 1884–1895 meant nothing else in New Hampshire, they were a decade marked by infamous railroad manipulation. The cast of involved parties divided into the hunters, among them the Boston & Lowell and the Boston & Maine, and the hunted—Concord RR, Northern RR, BC&M and small fry such as Manchester & Lawrence. Concord RR, once a marvel of financial strength and responsibility, endured a decade of peculations until about 1868, when certain rascals were turned out after being caught with their hands in the till, one of them Joseph A. Gilmore, of fortunately brief association with a BC&M committee back in 1857.

During this time the Boston & Lowell was a standard-bearer among railroads. It served the rich mill towns of the Merrimack River valley, bringing in coal and raw materials, hauling out finished products. Passenger business flourished. The Lowell System possessed the finest of motive power and rolling stock in all New England. Its strategy was to obtain

Boston & Lowell operated BC&M for the brief years 1884-1889. In a rare photo, here is "Ashland" bearing B&L lettering. *Edgar T. Mead*

control of the busy Northern RR, thus putting a squeeze on the Concord RR. Although the B&L and the Concord cancelled their operating agreement on March 1, 1883, citing "the embarrassment of continual litigation," the affair was far from concluded. Not illogically, on July 1, 1884, BC&M sought protection by leasing itself to the Lowell system for a period of 99 years. What did BC&M stockholders have to lose? In 36 years their dividends had been nil!

Boston & Lowell moved right in. An inventory in depth was taken, appraising every desk and spittoon, engine house and pile of parts. Action followed. The last remaining seven miles of iron rail were replaced. New "point" switches replaced ancient stub turnouts. Air brakes were installed. A new restaurant was built at Weirs to complement steamboat service. The more modern of the wood burners were converted to coal with new grates, cap stacks and extended smokeboxes, although a few puffed wood smoke for several years more on the up-country branches.

B&L went after passenger business with a vengeance, publishing tasteful timetables and issuing brochures luring city dwellers to its "White Mountains Division." Now the battle was joined in earnest, between Boston & Lowell in the west and Boston & Maine to the east. By trackage rights over Maine Central, B&M was thrusting long trains into Fabyans, and thirsted to serve resorts of the Presidential and Franconia Ranges where its arch rival was firmly entrenched.

Bell and Kimball, stockholders of BC&M, decided they could profit by arranging to break B&L's lease of the BC&M. Their first move was to offer stock control of BC&M to the B&L. It was a chancy thing but, as they foresaw, B&L refused the offer. Then they took to the courts. After a fight of several years' duration, B&L's lease of the BC&M was defeated in May 1889 (Dow vs. Northern RR). B&L, somewhat in desperation, had meanwhile leased itself to its former antagonist, the B&M. Under George C.

Lord and his Lawrence and Boston backers, B&M had already snapped up most of the eastern New Hampshire roads. The Bell-Kimball group had been quietly buying Concord RR stock during the years of financial squeeze, and on September 19, 1889, six months after the B&L lease had been cancelled, the General Court of New Hampshire blessed a union between Concord RR and Boston Concord & Montreal. Senator William E. Chandler was outraged. Leveling his ire at the Concord RR directors, he stormed, "as trustees of a living road, they bought a road which was almost a corpse and tied the living to the dead in order to revive the dying at the expense of the living, to their own vast personal profit." Who could have predicted that BC&M would now be wedded with the monster that sucked it dry of profits year after year?

In other ways, the merger was a blessing. When all the lawsuits started, Boston & Lowell ducked out of investing more money in its country cousin. But BC&M was in dire need of further modernization, as demands for greater speed and capacity mounted.

The new combination was called Concord & Montreal RR. Its president, Manchester tycoon Frederick C. Smyth, and Benjamin Kimball were (not surprisingly) named to the executive committee. The ornate 1886 depot at Concord became general headquarters. Figuring out the exchange of stock issues became a lawyers' field day. For example, one old share of "Boston, Concord & Montreal Old Stock" was exchanged for one new share of "Class 3 known as Boston Concord & Montreal Old Stock." Compounding

Spectacular bailout for stockholders in 1889 was the issue of Concord & Montreal Class 3 stock for BC&M "old stock." *Walter Wright*

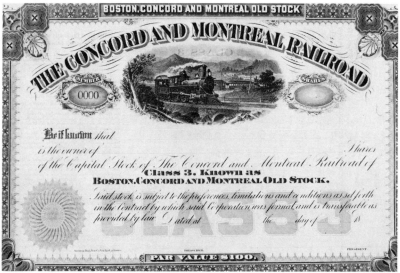

First train, Tilton to Belmont, in 1889 drew a melting pot of equipment: BC&M smoking car, B&L coach, Concord RR engine. *B. E. Naylor*

the confusion, "Boston, Concord & Montreal New Stock" was issued for "Old Stock (so-called) of the Boston Concord & Montreal RR." Came January 1, 1890, and the new Concord & Montreal company was under way.

A five-mile branch to connect Northern RR and C&M was built in 1892 between Tilton on C&M mainline and a point a mile south of Franklin, on the Northern. Although jointly owned by the two roads, this Franklin & Tilton RR was at first operated by the C&M and formally leased to C&M in 1895. It served a handful of mills at Franklin. In 1889, the four-mile Tilton & Belmont RR branch connected Tilton with a mill at Belmont, and a 17-mile Lake Shore line was constructed in 1890 between Lakeport and Alton Bay.

As logging moved further north, so followed the rails. Commencing in 1890 the twisty Whitefield & Jefferson was straightened and lengthened, and in July, 1899, trains ran all the way to Berlin Mills. A major engineering feature was the high bridge over the Androscoggin River at Gorham. Approaching Bowman Summit from the east, a grade of 1.97% was required. Even today, it challenges heavy diesel horsepower.

Profile & Franconia Notch RR trains at Bethlehem Jct., 1881 or thereabouts. The train at left for Bethlehem Street, the other for Profile House. *Walker Collection*

Like its B&L predecessor, C&M added to the flood of summer-vacation literature. Pictures of placid lakes alternated with views of misty mountains. Special excursion round-trip tickets tempted the travel-prone.

Wealthy families chartered private cars from the Wagner or Pullman Palace Car companies. During the high season, members of the fleet such as *Grasmere, Wanderer, Iolanthe* or *Pickwick* could be seen parked at Fabyans. Mann Boudoir Cars were attached to the 1 P.M. train from Boston, arriving Fabyans at 8:25 P.M.

A typical bargain excursion special would start from Boston and run up the B&M "Seashore Route," then up the steep Maine Central line *via* Bartlett to Crawford Notch and Fabyans, back *via* Plymouth and Concord to Boston, all for $12.00.

A more elaborate trip sold for $23.25. Leave Boston for Concord, then at Plymouth take the P.V. Branch train to North Woodstock. Stagecoach *via* the Flume to Profile House. Narrow-gauge Profile & Franconia Notch RR to Bethlehem Junction. Change at Bethlehem Junction for Fabyans. Change again for Base Station and change there for the summit of Mt. Washington. Return *via* Crawford Notch, Glen, and North Conway to Wolfeboro. Steamboat from Wolfeboro to Weirs. Return on C&M *via* Concord to Boston. What wouldn't we do to repeat that experience? It can be done in less than a day by auto, but without struggle and therefore without such wholesome respect for nature's mountains, forests and rivers.

Boston & Maine's lease of the Boston & Lowell in 1887 was just a starter. In 1889 B&M leased Northern RR and in 1893 the strategic Connecticut River RR. It meant that southern gateways were sealed off as far as the Concord & Montreal was concerned. Boston & Maine revenues were on the order of $15 million annually and net $5.7 million. The operating ratio was a healthy 65%. Cash dividends ranging between 6 and 9% had been paid regularly for over 40 years. The B&M owned 520 engines, 1,000 coaches, 11,000 freight cars, extensive repair shops and improved track. In 1895, the $100 par stock was selling at a substantial premium, and was traded for as high as 180. The future looked golden indeed.

On the other hand, Kimball, Tilton, Sulloway and others were opposed to the Boston colossus sneaking into New Hampshire. Growled Sulloway, "the Boston & Maine is known here as a notorious tax dodger."

But the B&M steamroller moved inexorably. Surrounded by B&M tracks, C&M was bound to capitulate sooner or later. Armed with its trusty 1842 New Hampshire charter, B&M leased the 440-mile Concord & Montreal on June 21, 1895—a final blessed relief for stockholders. Terms of the 91-year lease awarded them an amount equal to 7% per year. It assured not only cash but corporate improvements to buttress their equity.

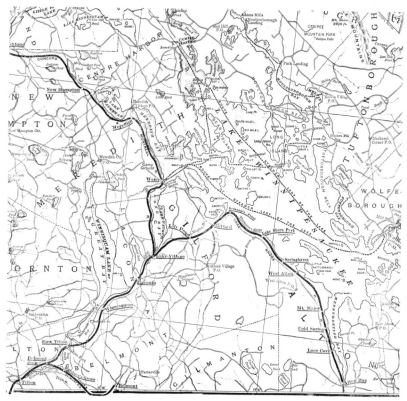

Lake Winnipesaukee map issued by C&M RR shows the branches, Lake Village to Alton Bay, Tilton to Belmont. *Edgar T. Mead*

For the original lines, the Concord and Boston, Concord & Montreal, a complete facelift was in prospect. Virtually all old BC&M engines had been junked before 1903. The newer C&M RR engines, such as the classy Atlantic 4—4—2 No. 33, were renumbered and reassigned. As veteran power and rolling stock faded away, facilities such as the Lake Village shops also were phased out. Using the excuse that parlor cars could go direct to Bethlehem or Profile House, B&M widened the narrow gauge and sold its rolling stock. (One of the engines wound up in Nantucket.) *Lady of the Lake* made her last voyage in 1893. After serving as a floating hotel for masons working on Benjamin Kimball's new "castle," she was sunk with full honors in Glendale Bay. (Still there, according to scuba divers.)

Fifty-six-pound rail was ripped out and replaced with heavier section. Creosoted ties and block signals were installed. Pleasant Greek Revival stations of the BC&M gave way to opulent stone edifices, of which the handsome structure at Laconia is an example. Within 15 years the B&M brownish-green stamp of uniformity was everywhere.

In 1902 the Concord & Montreal corporate shell was used to enter the traction business. It took over the 12-mile 42-inch gauge Concord streetcar system, shoved the old steam dummy engines aside, and converted to electricity. A 16-mile, standard-gauge inter-urban railway was built to Manchester, appropriately called the Concord & Manchester Electric RR. It was a relatively high-class affair with hourly service and suburban-style cars equipped with multiple unit control. A loop line at Centre and Franklin streets was added in 1910. The upper end of the streetcar line went to Contoocook River Park, a regular old-fashioned amusement park. On Penacook Lake C&M operated a fleet of small steamers led by the proud *Modena*. There was also a 15-inch gauge railway with a Cagney engine numbered 404.

The happy dream came to an end in 1913 when B&M passed a dividend for the first time since 1842! It had paid 3% in recent years, as high as 12% in 1864. One could argue with reason that the burden of carrying marginal lines like BC&M, as much as other factors, brought the entire enterprise to grief. The Concord & Montreal lease cost B&M all of $854,503 in 1914, an amount difficult—in retrospect—to justify because the eastern route *via* Intervale was regarded as mainline, not as part of the former BC&M.

Prof. George P. Baker of Harvard regarded B&M control as a necessary solution. Whether BC&M could have survived as an old-fashioned independent short line is certainly debatable. But overly-generous leases no doubt contributed to the later financial difficulties not only of the B&M, but the New Haven and New York Central systems as well.

An old BC&M observation car tags along after B&M Mogul No. 1481, used in early 20th-century operation on the tough 6% grade of the Fabyans-Base Station Branch. Uphill moves were made in reverse. *Doran Jones*

THE B&M LOOK—*Above:* The same Wing Road crosses the same track today, but all else has changed since this 1925 scene of a B&M Pacific 4—6—2 roaring south with a six-car Berlin train. *Norton D. Clark. Below:* Boston & Maine RR train No. 20, with Pacific No. 3663 on the head end, will leave Woodsville at 1:55 P.M. and make all stops to Concord, arriving at 4:40. Heaps of mail and express rode the train in 1939, when this picture was taken. *Edgar T. Mead*

The B&M strategy was to own as many of the securities of its leased lines as possible. After all, if a lease was generous, better to buy up the remaining shares, keep the cash at home and obtain various tax benefits. Before the B&M treasurer could buy all stray C&M stock shares, Concord & Montreal was officially consolidated with B&M as of January 1, 1919, under a court directive "to authorize the rehabilitation of the Boston & Maine RR." At that point the New Hampshire Public Service Board was to declare that "the corporate existence (of the C&M) is being continued only until the completion of all matters pertaining to the consolidation."

There was an operational flurry of revival in 1926, when Canadian Pacific bought a portion of the Connecticut & Passumpsic line between Newport, Vt., and Wells River, and obtained trackage rights over the former BC&M line from Woodsville south. CPR inaugurated a fast night sleeper train and a de luxe day train, *The Alouette,* that usually carried a fancy observation lounge car togged out with a brass rear platform. *Alouette* was a handsome replica of the good old days, but died after World War II.

As of 1975, local freight service operates between Concord and Meredith, N.H. There is no track between Plymouth and Blackmount (south of Woodsville). From Woodsville over the "Mountain Road" there is daily local service to Groteon, and a night freight to Berlin, mostly for the benefit of paper traffic. Maine Central freights still rumble through Fabyans, but the once-busy BC&M line from Wing Road is gone. Road-beds still exist: The best hiking trails are along the Profile & Franconia

THE B&M LOOK—*Below, left:* **With air pumps panting for breath, Boston & Maine Mogul 2—6—0 No. 207 waits for clearance at Warren Summit to assist another freight over the hill. About 1908.** *Below, right:* **Pacific No. 3655 hustles out of Fabyans with an eight-car consist of typical mid-'20s cars.** *Both from Doran Jones*

Notch RR, through Glencliff cut, and between Fabyans and Base Station. Hiking trails follow many of the log railroad lines in White Mountain National Forest.

The Mt. Washington RR flourishes, having added a new steam cog engine in 1972, the *Col. Teague.* The distinctive smokestacks and cabs proclaim their ancestral BC&M relationship. Steam trains at Clark's Trading Post and Loon Mountain provide the sounds, smell and action of the wood burning White Mountains log railroads.

Various combinations of highways follow the BC&M mainline from start to finish. Drive along some evening and imagine the sight of a double-headed freight train, brakemen frantically trying to control the heavy loads from their icy rooftop perches. Or the *Mountain Express* highballing along behind shiny *Chocorua,* showering wood sparks over the surrounding countryside, her fireman endlessly throwing chunks of cordwood into the fiery maw.

A long last whistle for the next station. The echoes gradually fade, and there is silence, with only the northern stars at night for company.

The End

**Elegant & impressive were Concord &
Montreal RR passes in its glittering twilight prior
to absorbtion by Boston & Maine RR.**
Edgar T. Mead

MEMORABILIA, ENGINE ROSTER, MAPS & MISCELLANY

Old tickets illustrating various corporate designations of the Boston, Concord & Montreal, also tickets of affiliates such as the Cog Railway and the Wells River Bridge Co. *Doran Jones*

"Chocorua," favorite BC&M engine built in the Lake Village shops sported high drivewheels for passenger assignments. *James Crimmins*

ROSTER OF BC&M ENGINES, 1848-1883
(All 4—4—0, except No. 6 0—4—0, No. 11 0—4—0 and No. 29 2—6—0)

BC&M	B&L	C&M	Name	Builder	No.
—	—	—	**Old Man of the Mountains**	Hinkley	162
	1	—	—	**Granite State**	Hinkley	176
2nd 1	103	64	2nd **Granite State**	Manchester	574
	2	—	—	**McDuffie**	Hinkley	225
	3	83	65	**Lady of the Lake**	Hinkley	187
	4	88	—	**Crawford**	Hinkley	226
—	—	—	**Josiah Quincy**	Souther	—
	5	—	—	**Peter Clark**	Hinkley	324
2nd 5	99	66	2nd **Peter Clark**	Hinkley	—
	6	—	—	**Paugus**	BC&M	—
2nd 6	100	67	**Whitefield**	Hinkley	—
	7	90	68	**Winnipiseogee**	Hinkley	440
	8	91	—	**Pehaungun**	Hinkley	441
—	—	—	**Moosilauk**	Hinkley	424
	9	95	—	**James N. Elkins**	Hinkley	473
	10	84	69	**Ahquedauken**	Hinkley	487
	11	—	—	**Pony**	Hinkley	357
2nd 11	107	70	**Littleton**	Manchester	804
	12	89	81	**Chocorua**	BC&M	—
	13	92	71	**Belknap**	Hinkley	—
	14	93	72	**Laconia**	Hinkley	—
	15	101	73	**Moosilauk**	Manchester	104
	16	102	74	**Franconia**	McKay & Aldus	
	17	96	75	**Lancaster**	Manchester	229

With a trainload of logs and a cabful of kids, second "Granite State" rests near Whitefield during the early 1890s. *Walter Fogg Collection*

Date	Drivers	Cylinders	Remarks
4/48	66	15 x 18 (I)	Burned 1857, repaired. Passenger
6/48	54	15 x 20	Wrecked 1873. Freight
6/73	n.a.	16 x 24	Ex-M&WR No. 3. Freight
2/49	54	15 x 20	Scrapped 1880. Freight. Shifter
7/48	60	15 x 18 (I)	Rebuilt 1878 as "Lady." Passenger
2/49	66	15 x 18 (I)	Scrapped 1889. Passenger
1850	66	— – — (I)	Burned 1857, scrapped. Passenger
8/51	66	15 x 24	Scrapped 1879(?). Freight
1879	n.a.	16 x 24	Freight
1852	54	— – —	Scrapped 1875(?). Gravel
1878	n.a.	16 x 24	Freight
4/53	60	15 x 24	Rebuilt 1873
5/53	60	16 x 20	Rebuilt 1871, scrapped 1889. Helper
2/53	60	15 x 24	Burned 1857, repaired, scrapped by 1887
9/53	66	15 x 24 (I)	Rebuilt 1872, scrapped 1889. Passenger
11/53	66	15 x 20 (I)	Rebuilt 1880. Passenger
3/52	54	12 x 20	Scrapped 1880(?). Gravel
4/80	n.a.	16 x 24	Freight
1856	66	15 x 22	First with air brakes, 1875. Passenger
1858	n.a.	15 x 24	Freight
1858	n.a.	15 x 24	Passenger
1/68	n.a.	16 x 24	Rebuilt 1887. Freight
1870	n.a.	16 x 24	Rebuilt 1882, 1887, after wrecks. Freight
5/70	n.a.	16 x 22	Rebuilt 1887. Helper

BC&M (1)	B&L (2)	C&M (3)	Name	Builder	No.
18	87	76	**Plymouth**	Manchester	341
19	110	77	**Ammonoosuc**	Manchester	342
20	94	78	**Carroll**	Manchester	366
21	111	62	**Gilford**	Manchester	465
22	85	79	**Coos**	Manchester	463
23	86	80	**Northumberland**	Manchester	464
24	112	—	**Tilton**	Manchester	549
25	97	61	**Fabyan**	Manchester	649
26	98	—	**Profile**	Manchester	650
27	104	63	**Stranger**	Manchester	657
28	105	60	**Tip Top**	Manchester	726
29	119	82	**Mt. Washington**	Manchester	731
30	106	83	**Ashland**	Manchester	750
31	108	84	**Bethlehem**	Manchester	818
32	113	85	**Lisbon**	Manchester	844
33	114	86	**Warren**	Manchester	928
34	109	87	**Haverhill**	Manchester	929
35	115	88	**Campton**	Manchester	1079
36	116	89	**Thornton**	Manchester	1080
37	117	90	**Canterbury**	Manchester	1135
38	118	91	**Wentworth**	Manchester	1136

(1) Carried BC&M numbers until 1884, also 1887-1889
(2) Carried Boston & Lowell numbers briefly, 1884-1887
(3) Carried Concord & Montreal numbers, 1889 until Boston & Maine System renumbering

Notes:

BC&M engines mostly scrapped by B&M, 1895-1903

Engines "Waumbek" and "Starr King" used on Brown Lumber Road, built as Whitefield & Jefferson RR 3 (1879) and 4 (1880), later C&M 93 and 94. Various Concord RR engines ran over BC&M; however, no records exist of these movements.

Profile & Franconia Notch RR (3 ft.) engines Nos. 1 "Echo" and 2 "Profile" 4—4—0 built by Hinkley, Nos. 1292 and 1285. No. 3 "Bethlehem" 0—6—0 saddle tank built by H. K. Porter, No. 431, June 1881. 12 x 16"

All cylinders outside frames unless indicated (I) for inside cylinders and drive cranks on front axle.

After Civil War, most BC&M passenger engines used 66-inch drive wheels, freight engines 60-inch.

The "Gilford," lettered for Concord & Montreal, shown with the extended smokebox and cap stack typical of BC&M engines converted to coal firing, about 1890 at Jefferson, N. H. *Walker Collection*
BC&M "Lancaster" was another of the few lucky wood burners successfully converted to coal, here balancing on a turntable, circa 1888. *Walker Collection*

Date	Drivers	Cylinders	Remarks
4/71	See	16½ x 24	Wrecked 1882. Rebuilt. Passenger
4/71	note	16½ x 24	Wrecked 1882. Rebuilt. Passenger
7/71	below	15 x 24	Before 1876 was "Mt.Washington." Passenger
5/72		16 x 24	Freight
6/72		14 x 22	Passenger
7/72		14 x 22	Passenger
4/73		16½ x 24	Scrapped 1889. Freight
4/74		16 x 22	Rebuilt, Manchester, 1889. Freight
4/74		16 x 22	Scrapped 1889. Passenger
9/74		16 x 24	Freight
5/75		16 x 24	Passenger
6/76		17 x 24	Mogul 2—6—0. Passenger
5/77		16 x 24	Freight
6/80		16 x 24	Passenger
12/80		16 x 24	Freight
5/81		16½ x 24	Freight
5/81		16 x 24	Freight
4/82		16 x 24	Assigned PVRR
5/82		16 x 24	Assigned PVRR
6/83		17 x 24	Freight
6/83		17 x 24	Freight

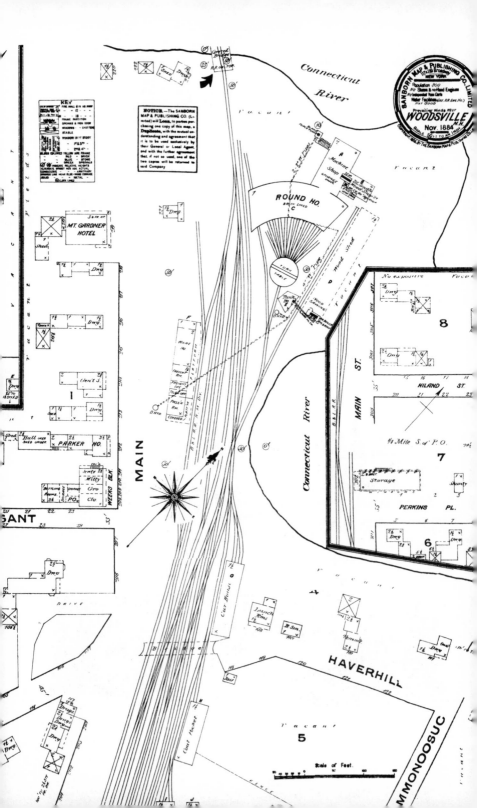

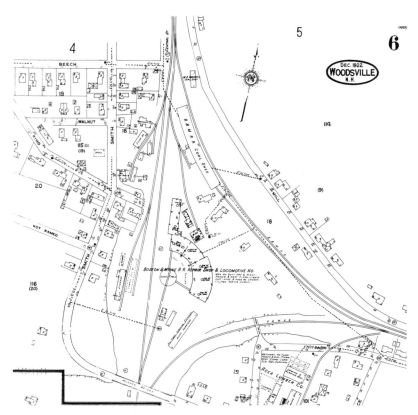

Facing page and below: **Steam, smoke and activity mark the old-time BC&M engine house at Woodsville, which also serviced motive power from Montpelier & Wells River and Connecticut & Passumpsic RRs. Machine shop was powered by a 75-horse steam engine; Mt. Gardner Hotel and Parker House boasted hydraulic elevators, the water pressure supplied by BC&M's Woodsville Aqueduct Co. Arrow at top of map points to location of double-deck bridge pictured on pages 22 and 37.** *Edgar T. Mead*

Above: **With the advent of larger engines, B&M abandoned the old, centrally-located facility for a newly built roundhouse in a wye southeast of town.** *Dartmouth College*

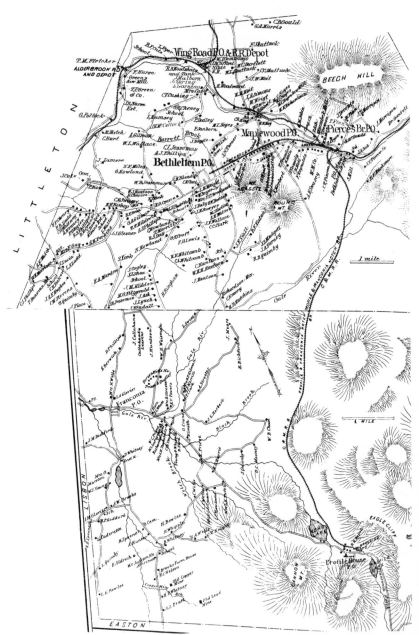

From Woodsville and Littleton the BC&M mainline followed the Ammonusuc River to Wing Road—where the branch to Lancaster and Groveton wyed north—and on to Fabyans. Narrow-gauge lines to Profile House and Bethlehem Street met at Bethlehem Junction, also called Pierce's Bridge, as on map above. Today skiers roar down Cannon Mt. and hikers scale Eagle Cliff oblivious to the vanished years of railroad transport into Franconia Notch. *Dartmouth College*

Ancient engines and cars decorate Civil War period freight bills for shipments over the Boston, Concord & Montreal. *John Brennan*

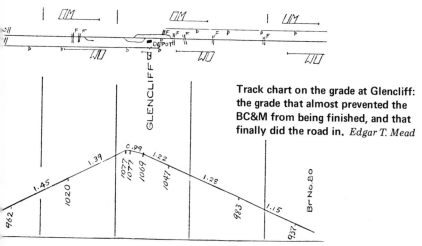

Track chart on the grade at Glencliff: the grade that almost prevented the BC&M from being finished, and that finally did the road in. *Edgar T. Mead*

Boston and Lowell Railroad.						Boston and Lowell Railroad.					
Northern Division. 260						260 *Northern Division.*					
Survey of wood bought of						*Survey* of wood bought of					
Me						*Me*					
P. O. Address,						P. O. Address,					
188 .						188 .					
Wood located at						Wood located at					
Pile No.	Length of Pile.	Height.	Length of Wood.	Kind.	Total Cords.	Pile No.	Length of Pile.	Height.	Length of Wood.	Kind.	Total Cords.

Under B&L control, BC&M wood agents beat the bushes for engine fuel. *D. Jones*

Boston, Concord & Montreal, White Mountains and Mount Washington Branch Railroads.

NORTHERN DIVISION. ——— TIME TABLE NO. 6.

IN EFFECT MONDAY, DEC. 31st, 1883.

FOR THE EXCLUSIVE USE AND INFORMATION OF EMPLOYES.

STATIONS (White Mountains Railroad):

- Wells River.
- Woodsville.
- White Mt. Transfer.
- Bath.
- Lisbon.
- No. Lisbon.
- South Littleton.
- Littleton.
- Alderbrook.
- Wing Road.
- Whitefield.
- Scott's.
- Lunenburg.
- Dalton.
- South Lancaster.
- Lancaster.
- Northumberland Falls.
- Groveton Junction.

STATIONS (Mt. Washington Branch Railroad):

- Wing Road.
- Bethlehem Junction.
- Twin Mountain.
- White Mt. House.
- Fabyan's.
- Base Mt. Washington.

W. A. STOWELL, Supt.
F. T. LEWIS, Ass't Supt.

B. H. CORNING, Div. Supt.

Note change in numbers of Trains and mistake them not. All first class trains are numbered 50 and upwards. At meeting, passing, and terminal stations, (Wing Road and Scotts to be considered terminal stations.) Train men MUST KNOW that all trains having right of road, or equal rights, have arrived or left, before allowing their trains to proceed. Train number 4 (Stock,) has right of road over train number 1 on White Mountain Road.

☞For General Rules see BOOK OF RULES AND REGULATIONS. Dated 1883.☜

In 1883, there was a Monday-only stock train from Lancaster, log trains between Fabyans and Wing Road, and P&O (later Maine Central) trains between Lunenburg, Wing Road and Fabyans before MC's own line was built. Instruction in small type at bottom admonishes employees to "Note changes in numbers of trains and mistake"